T0152103

The
Word of
Neville

A COMPILATION OF WISDOM
FROM
NEVILLE GODDARD

Collected and Edited by
Natalia Larson

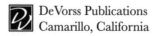

DeVorss Publications
Camarillo, California

The Word of Neville
A Compilation of Wisdom from Neville Goddard
Collected and Edited by Natalia Larson
Copyright © 2021

Library of Congress Catalog Number: 2021939694
First Printing, 2021

PRINT ISBN: 978-087516-920-0
EBOOK ISBN: 978-087516-921-7

DeVorss & Company, Publisher
PO Box 1389
Camarillo, CA 93012
www.devorss.com

Preface

All publishers can look back and reflect on certain books and authors that built the foundation of their publishing houses and established a legacy for their imprints. For DeVorss Publications, the author/publisher relationship with Neville Goddard has firmly been planted in their history. This long and prosperous relationship began with YOUR FAITH IS YOUR FORTUNE in 1941 in a small office near 9th and Grand in downtown Los Angeles, and continues to this day with books like THE POWER OF UNLIMITED IMAGINATION.

DeVorss Publications helped to provide Neville with the support he needed to share his message with the world. We will be forever grateful for his loyalty to us. Although Doug DeVorss (founder of DeVorss Publications in 1929) and Neville Goddard have long made their transitions, the impact of their vision remains alive today.

Neville Goddard
1905–1972

Neville Goddard was born in Barbados, West Indies. He was one son in a family of nine boys and one girl. At seventeen he moved to the United States to study drama. In 1932 he ended his theater career to devote his love to the studies of religion and spiritualism. He started lecturing in New York City and travelled throughout the country. Neville made his home in Los Angeles. In the late 1950s he gave a series of talks on television and for years he lectured to full house audiences at the Wilshire Ebell Theater in Los Angeles. His ten books were written over a period of thirty years. They deal with creative visualization and trans-formation of consciousness. Neville's books and lectures were very popular during his life. The popularity of Neville Goddard's work has resurfaced in current time because of the present theories of Quantum Physics and Reality Transurfing.

"Neville captured the sheer logic of creative mind principles. His work impacted me in a very profound way; in fact, he's been a great mentor to me."
—*Dr Wayne Dyer*

The
Word of
Neville

Foreword
by Margaret Ruth Broome

Neville was once described by Israel Regardie as "a dynamic, handsome and most charming personality. He has a winning smile thoroughly and completely disarming. His presentation of truth is forceful and sincere. Charged with feeling, and reflecting his own integrity and purposefulness, he communicates himself readily from the pulpit."

This is true. If you ever heard him speak you might not have agreed with him, in fact you might not have even understood him, but deep within you knew he was speaking the truth. Neville never "read" his lectures, never used notes, yet he knew and could quote the Bible verbatim. He never theorized, never speculated, but spoke only from his own personal experience.

Having attended Neville's lectures over the last ten years of his life, and having recorded them, I have transcribed, edited and compiled a group of twenty-four for the book IMMORTAL MAN (ISBN 9780875167237) as well as additional lectures from 1952 in another book, THE POWER OF UNLIMITED IMAGINATION (ISBN 9780875168791). Having discovered the truth hidden from the ages, Neville explains within these books the truth that will set you free. Allow me to share them with you, as he shared them with me.

"Imagination is more important than
knowledge. For knowledge is limited
to all we now know and understand,
while imagination embraces the entire
world, and all there ever will be
to know and understand."

—*Albert Einstein*

Prologue

The contents of this book are inspiring and thought-provoking notes that I jotted down while reading assorted books and lectures by Neville Goddard.

May these words resonate with the utmost meaning and purpose in your heart as well.

But most importantly, may they spark action in your life.

—Natalia Larson

Everything in life must
be an investment.

SOUND INVESTMENTS
1953

Order your life according to
your inner conversation.

CONTROL YOUR
INNER CONVERSATIONS
1971

Your world reflects your inner speech

CONTROL YOUR
INNER CONVERSATIONS
1971

Carry on a conversation
from the premise of the
wish fulfilled, a thing of
love, clothed in love, and
watch how things happen
in the world.

CONTROL YOUR
INNER CONVERSATIONS
1971

God's gift of mind and speech
is not of your outer speech,
but inner speech.

CONTROL YOUR
INNER CONVERSATIONS
1971

Conversation means
manner of life and
way of life.

CONTROL YOUR
INNER CONVERSATIONS
1971

Ask in faith
without doubting.

FEEL DEEPLY
1969

Assume your desire is now a
fact. Feel its substance and
reality. Then let your friends
see you in that state. They
are your living mirror. Now
persevere in that state and
do not turn away…

FEEL DEEPLY
1969

Dream better than the
best you know.

IMAGING CREATES REALITY
1967

Do nothing to obtain desire;
lead the actions in a normal,
natural manner.

IMAGING CREATES REALITY
1967

When ideas change so
do your intentions and
attitudes toward life.

THE SECRET OF CAUSATION
1969

"I am arresting the activity
within and silencing
the negatives that
stand before me."

THE SECRET OF CAUSATION
1969

It is impossible for a
thinking Being to know a
thought greater than self.

LIVE THE ANSWER NOW
1968

Recognition of truth will transform you from one who tries to make it so, to one who recognizes it to be so.

YOURS FOR THE TAKING
1967

Change your reaction to life to
change the environment and
your behavior. All your energy
flows from that state. Think
from that state.

CHANGING THE FEELING OF "I"
1953

Faith means the assurance
of things hoped for, the
evidence of things now seen.

FAITH
1968

We are the Operant Power.

A MOVEMENT WITHIN GOD
1967

Use the law of liberty and
persevere. Then you will be
blessed. Clothe yourself
in that feeling.

FEEL DEEPLY
1969

Your acceptance of
change will cause you
to modify the image of the
"you" that others hold.

THE LORD, OUR POTTER
1969

Closely weave a tapestry
of thought.

THE ULTIMATE SENSE
1969

Not a thing in this world
can be discarded, but it can
be revised and made into
your ideal image.

THE PRUNING SHEARS OF REVISION
1954

There is no other way
to save our self than to
save the real self.

THE PRUNING SHEARS OF REVISION
1954

There is a limit to opacity,
but no limit to translucency.

SPIRITUAL SENSATION
1969

Truth is ever-increasing
illumination.

TRUTH
1951

You cannot find a Cause
outside of your own
consciousness. Your world is
a grand mirror contstantly
telling you who you are.

REMAIN FAITHFUL TO YOUR IDEA
1948

Repent means radical change of attitude.

REPENTANCE, A GIFT FROM GOD
1972

Prayer is feeling the
wish fulfilled.

PRAYER
1945

Imagine fulfillment
of your desire; imagine
the action that follows
fulfillment of your desire.

REMAIN FAITHFUL TO YOUR IDEA
1948

Permeate the mind
with the feeling of the
desire fulfilled.

REMAIN FAITHFUL TO YOUR IDEA
1948

Creation is an act of mercy.

CREATION FAITH
1968

Generation to Regeneration.

CONCEPTION
1968

The only acceptable gift
is a joyful heart.

REMAIN FAITHFUL TO YOUR IDEA
1948

Never accept the suggestion
of lack.

REMAIN FAITHFUL TO YOUR IDEA
1948

Give yourself a
new concept of self.

REMAIN FAITHFUL TO YOUR IDEA
1948

Assume the desire and
give thanks.

AT YOUR COMMAND
1939

Persistent assumption will
harden into facts.

PERSISTENT ASSUMPTION
1968

Change is a characteristic of
a fourth dimension.

THINKING FOURTH DIMENSIONALLY
1948

All I need to do is ascend
to the level where the thing
desired is eternal and is
objectified by itself, and it will
appear as reality in the world.

REMAIN FAITHFUL TO YOUR IDEA
1948

The concept of yourself is the
cause of all the circumstances
in your life.

No One to Change But Self
1948

If you do not change from the
outside, it is because you have
not changed within.

NO ONE TO CHANGE BUT SELF
1948

Never entertain an undesirable feeling nor think sympathetically about wrong in any shape or form. We become what we contemplate.

FEELING IS THE SECRET
1951

We are incapable of
seeing other than through
the contents of our own
consciousness.

CONSCIOUSNESS IS THE
ONLY REALITY
1948

Never accept a
suggestion of lack.

REMAIN FAITHFULL TO YOUR IDEA
1948

If you do not forget,
then you have not forgiven.

REMAIN FAITHFUL TO YOUR IDEA
1948

Give yourself a new concept
for the old concept. Give up
the old concept completely.

REMAIN FAITHFUL TO YOUR IDEA
1948

If you walk faithful in a
high mood, there will be
no competition and
no opposition.

No on to Change but Self
1948

Desire is the mainspring
of action.

OUT OF THIS WORLD
1949

Use your imagination lovingly
on behalf of everyone and
believe in its reality.

WALK ON WATER
1968

You are the reality that is called imagination.

OUT OF THIS WORLD
1949

Time and Space are
conditions of thought.

PRAYER, THE ART OF BELIEVING
1945

To reach a higher level of being, you must assume a higher concept of yourself.

THE POWER OF AWARENESS
1952

Break the spell and
walk by faith.

ALL THINKS ARE POSSIBLE
1969

Do not entertain the feeling
of regret or failure, for
frustration and detachment
from our objective results
in disease.

FEELING IS THE SECRET
1951

Use your imagination in a state of bliss

THE HIDDEN CAUSE
1969

Don't analyze yourself, for if
you do, you will miss the mark.

WALK ON WATER
1968

To worry about what you
may have done is a waste
of your creative power.

WALK ON WATER
1968

Do not dwell within the
imperfections of yourself
or others.

FEELING IS THE SECRET
1951

Imagine in terms of
clarity and form.

WHAT ARE YOU DOING?
1967

Always think of clarity and form, for as you do, you are.

WHAT ARE YOU DOING?
1967

Put all your energies
into clarity and form.

WHAT ARE YOU DOING?
1967

When you discover the truth,
you cannot hurt another.

THE INCARNATE REVELATION
1969

Imagination is the
only foundation.

No Other Foundation
1968

A change of impression results
in a change of expression.

FEELING IS THE SECRET
1951

That which stirs us
to a higher state is our
teacher and healer.

BE WHAT YOU WISH,
BE WHAT YOU BELIEVE
1951

Never lose sight of the
power of Light that
is within you.

BY IMAGINATION WE BECOME
1951

The basic Truth of Life is
the offspring of Love.

BY IMAGINATION WE BECOME
1951

Determined Imagination
is the beginning of all
successful operations.

BY IMAGINATION WE BECOME
1951

Prayer is surrender. It means
abandoning oneself to the
feeling of the wish fulfilled.

ANSWERED PRAYER
1951

Life is not a struggle,
but a surrender.

PRAYER
1951

The great secret to
success is controlled
imagination and will.

BE WHAT YOU WISH,
BE WHAT YOU BELIEVE
1951

Dignity indicates that you
hear the greater music of
Life and move to a tempo
of its deeper meaning.

REVEALED TRUTH
1969

Feeling and imagination
are the senses by which
we perceive the beyond,
where knowledge ends and
imagination begins.

FEELING IS THE SECRET
1951

In the creation of a new life, we must begin with our own individual regenerations.

AFFIRM THE REALITY OF
YOUR OWN GREATNESS
1951

Our thoughts are the natural
outpouring of ideas.

AFFIRM THE REALITY OF
YOUR OWN GREATNESS
1951

An old idea is forgotten if it is
crowded out by new ideas.

AFFIRM THE REALITY OF
YOUR OWN GREATNESS
1951

All your present beliefs, fears and limitations are weights that bind you to your present level of consciousness.

AWAKENED IMAGINATION
1954

The greatest command
ever recorded is found
in a few simple words,
"Let there be light."

AT YOUR COMMAND
1939

Claim yourself to be the
thing you desire. Claim it in
consciousness, not in works,
and consciousness will reward
you with your claim.

AT YOUR COMMAND
1939

The door is your
consciousness.

YOUR FAITH IS YOUR FORTUNE
1941

Where knowledge ends,
imagination begins.

FEELING IS THE SECRET
1951

The healing touch is
in the attitude.

FEELING IS THE SECRET
1951

Faith is loyalty to
unseen Reality.

FAITH
1968

Detachment is to separate our
present reaction to life and
attach our aim to life.

Fundamentals
1953

Our inner states attract
our outer self.

FUNDAMENTALS
1953

How would I feel if I were free? The moment you sincerely ask this question the answer comes. As doubts vanish you can feel the I Am of this.

YOUR FAITH IS YOUR FORTUNE
1941

Learn to count on your
true self.

ALL THINGS EXIST
1968

All that you behold, though
it appears without, is within.
It is in our imagination.

ALL THINGS EXIST
1968

There is no limit to expansion
and luminosity.

ALL THAT YOU BEHOLD
1969

Truth is an ever-increasing
illumination.

TRUTH
1951

Make the *then* now, and
the *there* here.

CONSCIOUSNESS
1948

The conflicts raging in my
world simply mirror the
conflicts raging in me.

THE SIGNS OF THE END
1967

All day long, a miracle goes
on in your body.

AWAKE O SLEEPER
1968

Except by Love we
cannot truly live at all.

By Imagination We Become
1969

Dream nobly!

THE VALUE OF DREAMS
1969

Your inward conversations
are the breeding ground of all
your future action.

THE POWER OF UNLIMITED IMAGINATION:
THE PERFECT WILL OF GOD
1952

It is your mood which
describes your fortune,
not your fortune that
describes your mood.

THE GAME OF LIFE
1969

Desire is your mainspring of action, for you cannot move without desire.

THE POWER OF UNLIMITED IMAGINATION:
DESIRE
1952

There is only one Cause, and that is consciousness. Your consciousness is the center from which your world mirrors and echoes the state you presently occupy.

THE POWER OF UNLIMITED IMAGINATION:
YOUR INFINITE WORTH
1952

Learn to adore your humanity,
your spirit of Life.

FOLLOW THE PATTERN
1968

Anxiety has no creative power.

THE POWER OF UNLIMITED IMAGINATION:
THE PERFECT WILL OF GOD
1952

Awaken to the discovery that
everything you seek in time is
contained within you.

THE POWER OF UNLIMITED IMAGINATION:
THE PEARL OF GREAT PRICE
1952

You and all imagination
are the sum total of your
reaction to life.

THE POWER OF UNLIMITED IMAGINATION:
SELF-REMEMBERING
1951

Consciousness is the only
substance and the only Cause
of the phenomena of life;
therefore, it is impossible for
change to occur until there is a
change in consciousness.

THE POWER OF UNLIMITED IMAGINATION:
YOUR DESIRE
1952

No one can grow without
outgrowing.

THE POWER OF UNLIMITED IMAGINATION:
THE WINE OF ETERNITY
1952

Discouraged people are solely
in need of the inspiration
of higher ideals.

AFFIRM THE REALITY OF YOUR OWN GOODNESS
1951

As your belief in yourself
grows, your heart will
find peace.

THE POWER OF UNLIMITED IMAGINATION:
YOUR PERSONAL AUTOBIOGRAPHY
1952

Your destination is always
reached by an internal
direction.

THE POWER OF UNLIMITED IMAGINATION:
YOUR PERSONAL AUTOBIOGRAPHY
1952

All conceptions are limitations
of the conceiver.

YOUR FAITH IS YOUR FORTUNE
1941

YOUR FAITH IS YOUR FORTUNE
978-087516-078-8

IMMORTAL MAN
978-087516-723-7

THE NEVILLE READER
978-087516-811-1
Includes: Seedtime and Harvest

THE POWER OF
UNLIMITED IMAGINATION
978-087516879-1
A Collection of Neville's
1952 San Francisco Lectures

Natalia Larson

Natalia Larson has an abiding passion for the world's religions, especially those that espouse the expansion of consciousness through various practices. As she travelled to Spain to attend the Parliament of the World's Religions, she met Robert Burns, a mind/body fitness devotee who was pivotal in her personal journey. She holds a BS in Liberal Sciences; is a licensed real estate agent and has expertise in sales and management. Her career has taken her across the United States and to Canada and Europe. Active in physical fitness and health, she enjoys preparing gourmet meals. She currently makes her home in Orange County California.